CRUEL CRIMES

by William Anthony

BEARPORT
PUBLISHING

Minneapolis, Minnesota

Credits

Images are courtesy of Shutterstock.com. With thanks to Getty Images, Thinkstock Photo, and iStockphoto. Front Cover – Macrovector, Laborant, ZARIN ANDREY, Tereshchenko Dmitry. 4–5 – javarman, SofiaV, lady–luck, illustrissima. 6–7 – Puslatronik, proslgn, SimpleThings, waewkid. 8–9 – Morphart Creation, guidopiano, Dm_Cherry. 10–11 – Andrey Burmakin, owncham, Kachalkina Veronika, Fun Way Illustration. 12–13 – New Africa, artemiya, witsanu deetuam. 14–15 – Dmitrijs Mihejevs, meunierd, German Vizulis, Krasovski Dmitri. 16–17 – Olha Zinovatna, JIR Moronta, Steve Allen. 18–19 – vectorlab2D, ZARIN ANDREY. 20–21 – Photo–Art–Lortie, Steve Bruckmann, BlueRingMedia. 22–23 – givaga, Luis Louro, Bobby Stevens Photo, Phant, GoodStudio . 24–25 – tynyuk, Sergii Gnatiuk, Marina Datsenko, Sergey Nesterchuk. 26–27 – digitmilk, kittirat roekburi, Zoe Esteban, Raland, Everett Collection. 28–29 – Tiko Aramyan, Krakenimages.com, SHCHERBAKOV SERHII, TheLiftCreativeServices, Tomacco. 30 – Tinnakorn jorruang.

Bearport Publishing Company Product Development Team

President: Jen Jenson; Director of Product Development: Spencer Brinker; Managing Editor: Allison Juda; Associate Editor: Naomi Reich; Associate Editor: Tiana Tran; Senior Designer: Colin O'Dea; Associate Designer: Elena Klinkner; Associate Designer: Kayla Eggert; Product Development Specialist: Anita Stasson

Library of Congress Cataloging-in-Publication Data is available at www.loc.gov or upon request from the publisher.

ISBN: 979-8-88822-024-5 (hardcover)
ISBN: 979-8-88822-214-0 (paperback)
ISBN: 979-8-88822-339-0 (ebook)

For more information, write to Bearport Publishing, 5357 Penn Avenue South, Minneapolis, MN 55419.

CONTENTS

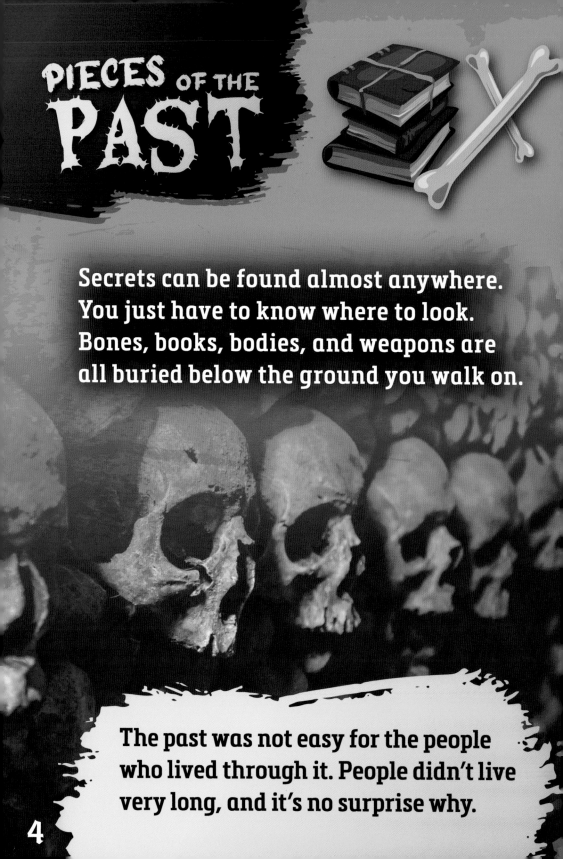

PIECES OF THE PAST

Secrets can be found almost anywhere. You just have to know where to look. Bones, books, bodies, and weapons are all buried below the ground you walk on.

The past was not easy for the people who lived through it. People didn't live very long, and it's no surprise why.

Disease and war were everywhere. People could be punished for crimes they did not do. No one was ever far from disaster.

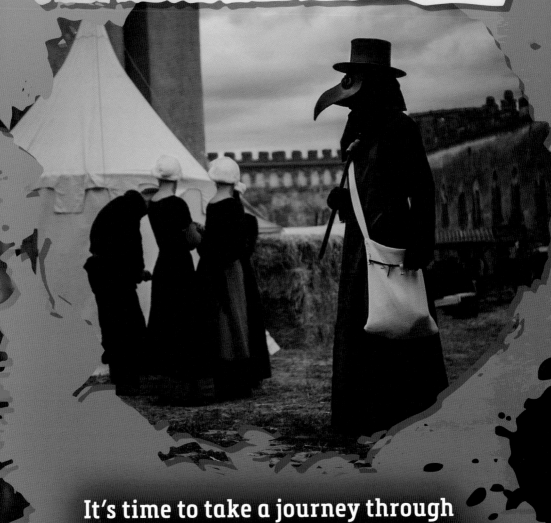

It's time to take a journey through the past. Be prepared for cruel events and horrible punishments as we enter the hideous history of crime.

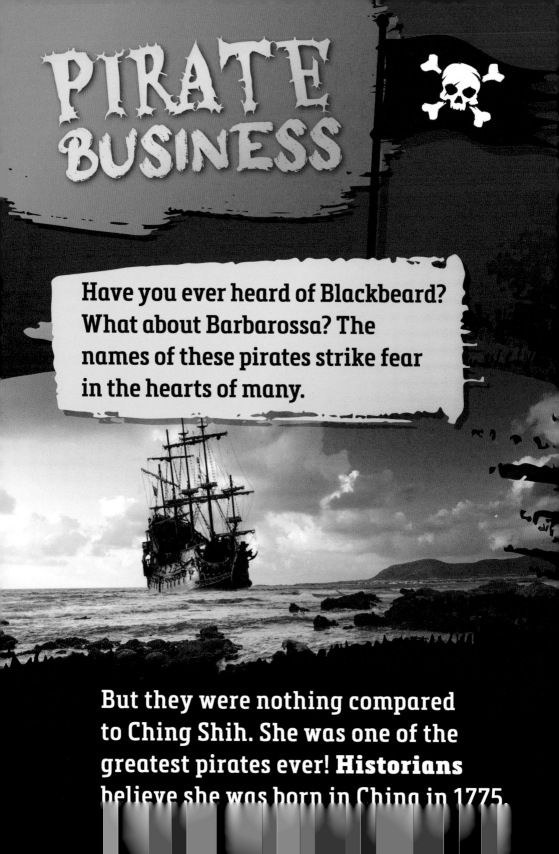

PIRATE BUSINESS

Have you ever heard of Blackbeard? What about Barbarossa? The names of these pirates strike fear in the hearts of many.

But they were nothing compared to Ching Shih. She was one of the greatest pirates ever! **Historians** believe she was born in China in 1775.

Ching Shih led a group of ships called the Red Flag **Fleet.** Her fleet robbed many towns and even other ships.

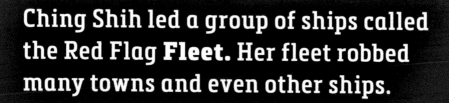

Ching Shih made lots of rules for the pirates who worked for her. Many of her rules protected women. If the crew didn't follow the rules, they would have parts of their bodies chopped off!

THE UNKNOWN KILLER

In 1888, there was a killer on the loose in London, England. He was called Jack the Ripper.

Jack the Ripper was never caught. But he was so famous that some people are still trying to figure out who he was!

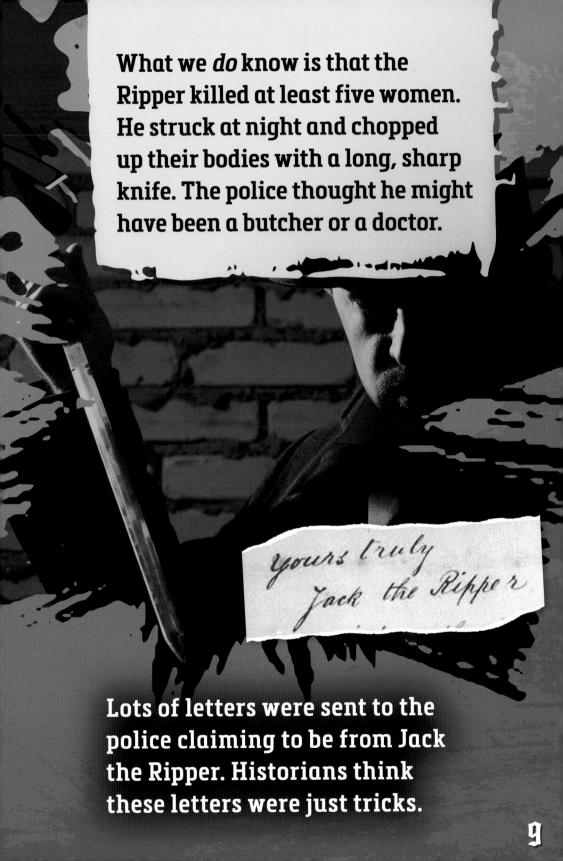

What we *do* know is that the Ripper killed at least five women. He struck at night and chopped up their bodies with a long, sharp knife. The police thought he might have been a butcher or a doctor.

yours truly
Jack the Ripper

Lots of letters were sent to the police claiming to be from Jack the Ripper. Historians think these letters were just tricks.

STEALING FROM THE RICH

Robin Hood was an **outlaw** who may have lived in England as early as the 14th century. He was said to live in Sherwood Forest with other outlaws called the Merry Men.

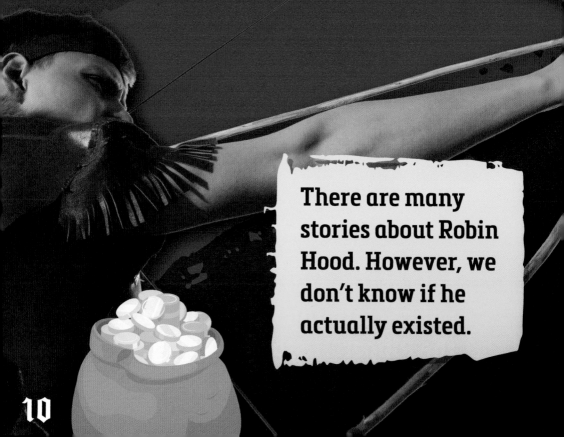

There are many stories about Robin Hood. However, we don't know if he actually existed.

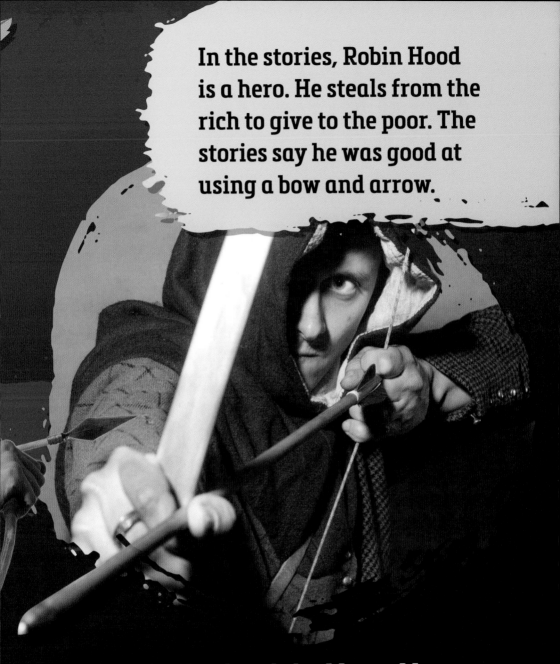

In the stories, Robin Hood is a hero. He steals from the rich to give to the poor. The stories say he was good at using a bow and arrow.

If Robin Hood and the Merry Men did exist, they were probably more **violent** than in the stories. In some cases, the Merry Men may have killed people. That's not heroic!

THE SCENE OF THE CRIME

There was once a real-life version of Sherlock Holmes. His name was Edmond Locard and he lived in France. He changed the way people solved crimes.

Locard used science. He found clues instead of only listening to **witnesses.**

He spent lots of time **researching** fingerprints. If someone left prints at one of his crime scenes, police could often find the **criminal**.

Locard also learned that things such as makeup and hairs can be passed between two people when they touch.

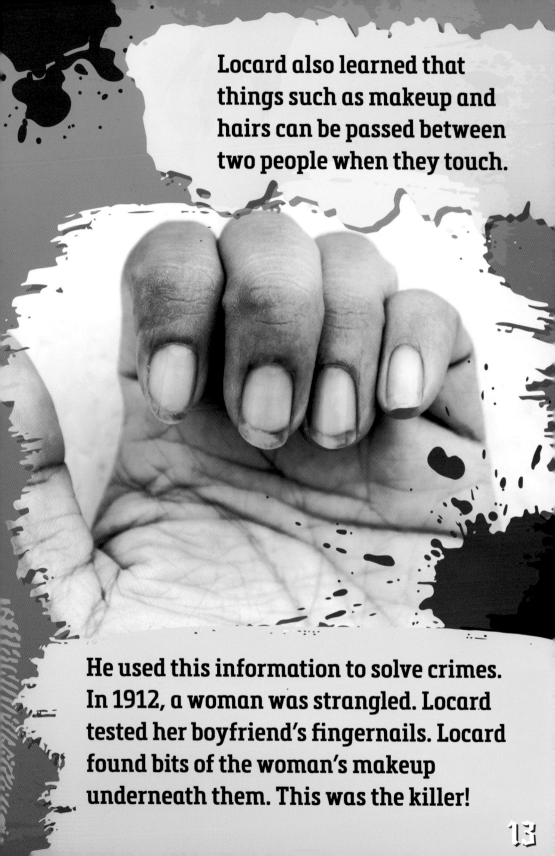

He used this information to solve crimes. In 1912, a woman was strangled. Locard tested her boyfriend's fingernails. Locard found bits of the woman's makeup underneath them. This was the killer!

THE WILD, WILD WEST

In the late 19th century, the western parts of North America became known for crime. Many people ignored laws and did bad things.

Police had guns. Outlaws had guns. Ordinary people had guns. It was no wonder there were lots of gunfights in the Wild West!

There was a famous group of outlaws called the Wild Bunch. It was led by Butch Cassidy. The Wild Bunch got money by robbing trains and banks.

Billy the Kid was one of the most well-known gunmen in the Wild West. One time, he was caught by police. But he got free and went on the run. He was finally found again and shot.

TICK, TICK, BOOM

One of the most famous criminals in Britain's history didn't even get the chance to commit his crime. He was named Guy Fawkes.

NOV 5

Fawkes planned to blow up a government building in London. His criminal group tried to put gunpowder underneath the building. They set the **plot** for November 5, 1605.

However, someone tipped off the government. Guy Fawkes was arrested, taken away, and killed!

Now, the people of Britain remember him every November 5th. People light big fires and set off fireworks.

BIG EARS

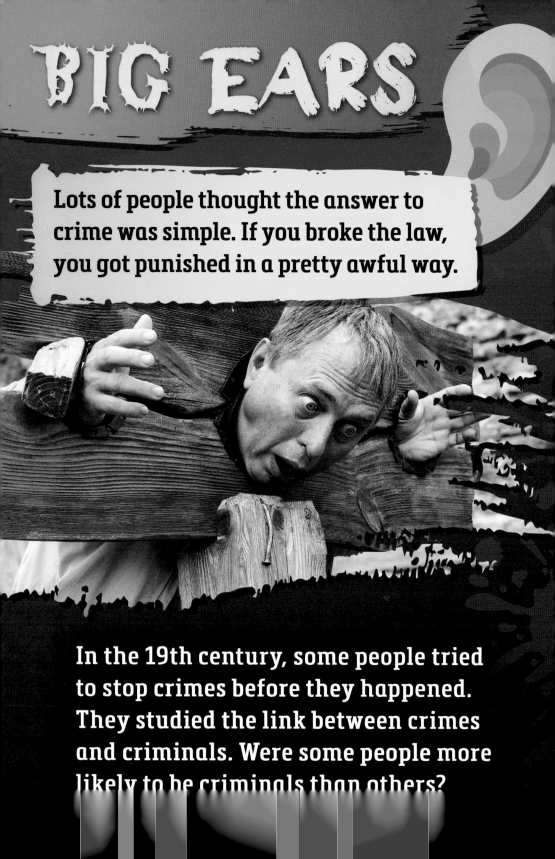

Lots of people thought the answer to crime was simple. If you broke the law, you got punished in a pretty awful way.

In the 19th century, some people tried to stop crimes before they happened. They studied the link between crimes and criminals. Were some people more likely to be criminals than others?

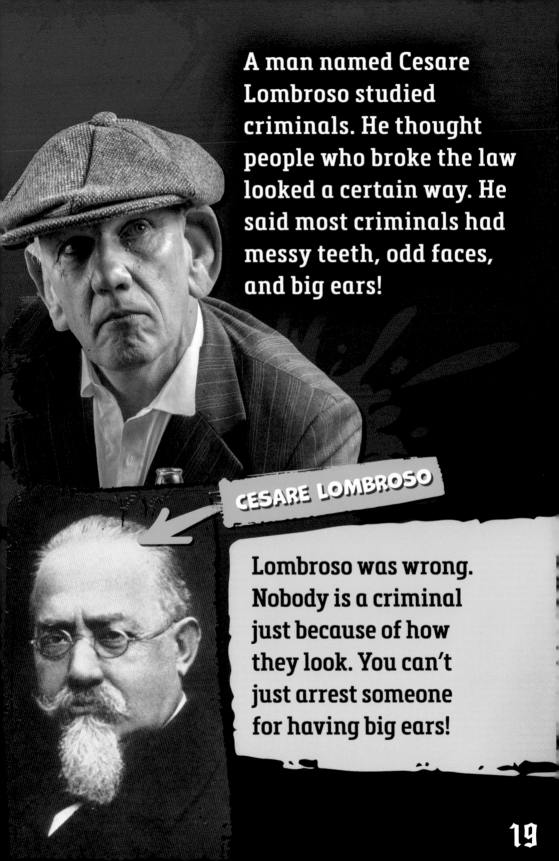

A man named Cesare Lombroso studied criminals. He thought people who broke the law looked a certain way. He said most criminals had messy teeth, odd faces, and big ears!

CESARE LOMBROSO

Lombroso was wrong. Nobody is a criminal just because of how they look. You can't just arrest someone for having big ears!

ON THE RUN

Bonnie Parker and Clyde Barrow met in Texas in 1930 and fell in love. Clyde was arrested for **burglary** soon after. Bonnie helped him escape.

Bonnie and Clyde ran away together. For two years, the couple robbed small businesses and banks. They killed anyone who got in their way.

Life on the run wasn't as exciting as it might sound. Bonnie and Clyde had to take baths in rivers and eat food from cans. They were always on the lookout.

Police finally caught Bonnie and Clyde while the couple was visiting a friend. The police fired at Bonnie and Clyde's car and shot them to death.

ROMAN RULES

Ancient Rome wasn't a place you'd want to be. Pee and poop rained down from windows. At night, people would be attacked and robbed. It was not the nicest place.

Millions of people lived in Ancient Rome and there was lots of crime. However, the Romans didn't have a police force!

Instead, they had people called vigiles. These watchmen usually tried to stop fires, but they also looked out for crime. Some vigiles were good people. Others were not.

There are stories of vigiles doing crimes themselves. Some vigiles once went around the city stealing during a huge fire!

THE ART OF THE CON

Victor Lustig was known as one of the greatest **con** men of all time. However, there is no record of a man by that name being born.

We know the man existed, but he had at least 47 different names throughout his life. He changed his name often to trick people into giving him money.

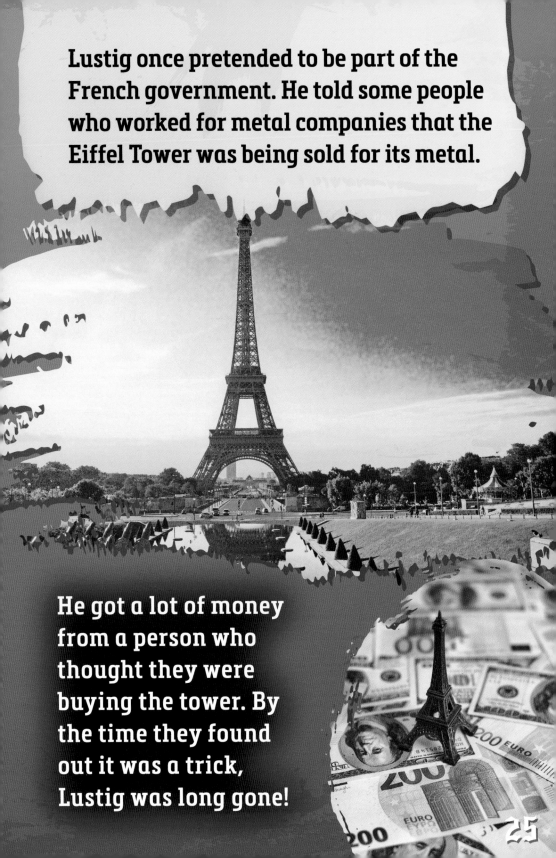

Lustig once pretended to be part of the French government. He told some people who worked for metal companies that the Eiffel Tower was being sold for its metal.

He got a lot of money from a person who thought they were buying the tower. By the time they found out it was a trick, Lustig was long gone!

WITCH HUNT

Not everyone found **guilty** of a crime has done one.

ENTERING
EST. 1626
SALEM

In the late 1600s in Salem, Massachusetts, many people were very afraid of witches. Three young girls said they had been cursed by witches. Being a witch

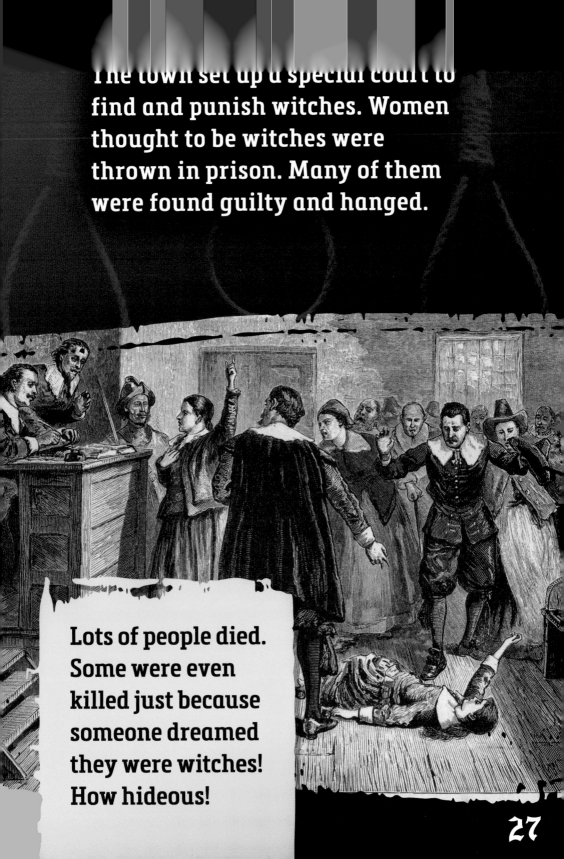

The town set up a special court to find and punish witches. Women thought to be witches were thrown in prison. Many of them were found guilty and hanged.

Lots of people died. Some were even killed just because someone dreamed they were witches! How hideous!

TERRIBLE TORTURE

Today, lots of different things stop people from doing crimes. But cameras and alarms weren't around long ago.

Instead, when people were caught they were given horrible punishments.

RED HOT

People might have been forced to hold a red-hot iron bar. If their hands healed after three days, they were not guilty.

WORK HARD, OR ELSE

Prisoners were forced to work. They were beaten if they didn't work hard enough.

CHOP, CHOP

People were sometimes punished by having body parts cut off. Someone caught stealing might have their hand chopped off.

HIDEOUS HISTORY

Take a deep breath. Let your heart slow back down again. The past was a scary place to be, but you are not there now.

A life of crime didn't end well for many criminals. Their horrible stories go to show crime doesn't pay!

GLOSSARY

burglary the act of stealing something

con something misleading or deceptive

criminal a person who is thought to have done a crime

fleet a group of ships under the control of one person

guilty responsible for a bad action or wrongdoing

historians people who study what happened in the past

outlaw someone who lives a life that doesn't follow the rules

plot a secret plan

researching finding out about a particular thing

violent especially harmful or destructive

witnesses people who saw something happen

INDEX

READ MORE

Bragg, Georgia. *Caught! Nabbing History's Most Wanted.* New York: Crown Books for Young Readers, 2019.

Faust, Daniel R. *The Real Story Behind the Wild West (The Real Story: Debunking History).* New York: PowerKids Press, 2020.

Gunasekara, Mignonne. *Death by Awful Accidents (Disastrous Deaths).* Minneapolis: Bearport Publishing Company, 2022.

LEARN MORE ONLINE

1. Go to **www.factsurfer.com** or scan the QR code below.

2. Enter "**Cruel Crime**" into the search box.

3. Click on the cover of this book to see a list of websites.